KB076922

# Learning Grammar with Drama
# 1

# Learning Grammar with Drama 1

**발 행** | 2023년 12월 15일

**저 자** | Dinka Hernández Avilés

**펴낸이** | 한건희

**펴낸곳** | 주식회사 부크크

**출판사등록** | 2014.07.15(제2014-16호)

**주 소** | 서울특별시 금천구 가산디지털1로 119 SK트윈타워 A동 305호

**전 화** | 1670-8316

**이메일** | info@bookk.co.kr

ISBN | 979-11-410-6015-2

www.bookk.co.kr

# SPECIAL THANKS

For starters, my wonderful mother, Veronica, who has never stopped supporting me and encouraging me. I would not be where I am today if it was not for her.

To my grandmothers, Dinka and Rosa, who are no longer physically with me but I know their souls walk with me everyday.

To my amazing friends, Paula, Sofia, Maria, Megan and my friends in Chile who stayed next to me at my lowest moments.

To my Professors; Teresa and Sujeong, who showed me the fascinating world of Drama in the classroom.

To my students, you are the reason I love my job: Kate, James, Flora, Juwon, Taekyeon, Tony, Ah-In, Ha-Im, Jiyu, Jayden, Daisy, Ella, Elina, Luke, Seoa, Simba, Chaeny, big Luke, Charlotte, Bella, Ted, Minchan, Dae, Sofia, Seoho. Thank you for allowing me to be your teacher and for always making me part of your adventures.

To Lizzy for her support and for valuing my skills and knowldege.

To my Master's degree classmates; Elena, Jiseon and Swapna. Thank you for the laughs and the reflective conversations.

Last but not least, I want to thank me; for never giving up despite all the storms unleashed in my way, for believing in myself that I can make things happen, and for becoming the woman I always dreamed to be.

# TABLE OF CONTENTS

Why Learning Grammar with Drama?                          P.7

Message to Educators                                       P.8

About the Author                                           P.8

Syllabus                                                   P. 9-12

Unit 1: ...and Action! (Verbs)                             P. 13-15

Unit 2: Pronouns and sentence structure                   P. 16-18

Unit 3: Nouns in the sentence                              P. 19-21

Unit 4: Let's use adjectives!                              P. 22-24

Unit 5: Using Articles                                     P. 25-27

Unit 6: 1, 2, 3... Singulars and plurals                   P. 28-30

Unit 7: The special be (verb 'be')                         P. 31-33

Unit 8: Wh Questions                                       P. 34-37

Final Projects Ideas                                       P. 38-44

*Appendices:*

Unit 1: Let's Practice! -  Verb Charades:                  P. 45- 53

Unit 5: Warm Up- Dialogues                                 P. 54

Unit 5: Let's Practice! - Article Hunt (Scripts)           P. 56- 60

Unit 6: Warm Up- Singular/ Plural Relay List               P. 62

Self-Evaluation                                            P.64

Epilogue                                                   P. 67

# INTRODUCTION:
# WHY LEARNING GRAMMAR WITH DRAMA?

Learning grammar can be quite a monotonous and tortous experience for most students since they have to learn all these bunch of rules and uses in a whole different language. However, it can also present a difficulty for teachers who love bringing interaction and dynamism to the classroom, which most of the time is hard since they have to follow a book that only allows them to work in a pretty conventional classroom setting: the teacher in the front, the students sitting and working on their books.

Therefore in my vast experience as an English teacher, especially as an English teacher in South Korea, along with my academic knowledge acquisition, I have come up with the idea that it is always possible to bring fun into the classroom, no matter what age of the students.

Thus, I have developed this book series as a way to aid teachers to bring that spark into the classroom and make something that seems so boring and challenging, into something that can also be exciting and fun.

I hope you have fun using this book as much as I did writing it.

# MESSAGE TO EDUCATORS

My dear fellow teachers:

I hope that when you get in the classroom you can feel that there, in front of your eyes, lays the future. All those lovely little monkeys are the tomorrow and what you do in the classroom does impact what they will become.

I hope you know that you are forming people and not machines, and as so I hope you can find value in such resources as imagination, creativity and play. That is why I created this book, to make it slightly easier for you to use these skills as assets for conveying knowledge. I truly hope you can get fascinated with the outcomes as I did when I started to put this method into practice.

I wish you the best of luck!

# ABOUT THE AUTHOR

Dinka Yolanda Hernández Avilés is a Chilean psychologist, who has been working in the education field for 6 years. She has experience teaching languages (English and Spanish) in her country, Chile, as well as in South Korea and China. She has also worked as a content writer for a humanitarian company in Turkey, as well as a volunteer psychologist at YMCA-Europe offering services for victims of the Russian- Ukrainian conflict. Currently, she is pursuing her Master's degree in ESL at IGSE in South Korea.

# SYLLABUS

| Unit 1 | ...and action! (verbs) | Goal | |
|---|---|---|---|
| Warm-Up | Look and write | • For students to activate prior knowledge.<br>• For students to practice the written form of the verbs. | |
| Let's Practice! | Verb Charades | • For students to practice the spoken form of verbs in a memorable way. | |
| Your Turn! | Action Verbs Skit | • For students to make use of verbs in an active and creative way. | |

| Unit 2 | Pronouns and sentence structure. | Goal | |
|---|---|---|---|
| Warm-Up | Read and Identify | • For students to review prior content.<br>• For students to practice subjet pronouns recognition. | |
| Let's Practice! | Make Sentences | • For students to practice correct use of subject pronouns.<br>• For students to practice writing. | |
| Your Turn! | Creation Time | • For students to produce oral sentences by using the proper subjective pronouns. | |

# SYLLABUS

| Unit 3 | Nouns in the sentence. | Goal |
|---|---|---|
| Warm-Up | Look and Identify | • For students to recognize basic nouns.<br>• For students to practice the written form of basic nouns. |
| Let's Practice! | Nouns Alphabet | • To challenge students to practice different nouns orally. |
| Your Turn! | Nouns Acrostic Poem | • To consolidate knowledge by producing a creative writing task. |

| Unit 4 | Let's use adjectives! | Goal |
|---|---|---|
| Warm-Up | Adjective Transformation | • For students to activate prior knowledge.<br>• For students to practice the written form of adjectives.<br>• For students to practice the use of longer-detailed sentences. |
| Let's Practice! | Adjective Swap | • For students to practice proper use of adjectives. |
| Your Turn! | Adjective Storytelling | • For students to consolidate knowledge by producing a task using adjectives. |

# SYLLABUS

| Unit 5 | Using Articles. | Goal |
|---|---|---|
| Warm-Up | Dialogues | • For students to remember prior contents.<br>• For students to identify the correct use of articles. |
| Let's Practice! | Article Hunt | • For students to cognitively make use of articles. |
| Your Turn! | Character Descriptions | • To use articles in a creative, more natural context. |

| Unit 6 | 1, 2, 3... Singulars and plurals. | Goal |
|---|---|---|
| Warm-Up | Singular/ Plural Relay | • For students to practice identifying singular and plural nouns correctly. |
| Let's Practice! | Singular/ Plural Mix-Up | • For students to gain further confidence in recognizing proper use of singular and plural nouns.<br>• For students to practice writing. |
| Your Turn! | Plural Storytelling | • For students to consolidate the grammar point knowledge in a creative way. |

# SYLLABUS

| Unit 7 | The special be (verb 'be'). | Goal |
|---|---|---|
| Warm-Up | Guess the Role | • To activate prior knowledge.<br>• To practice the correct use of verb "be" in an engaging- verbal way.<br>• To enhance confidence by interacting using the target language. |
| Let's Practice! | Character Descriptions | • To recapitulate prior contents.<br>• To gain further practice using this sentence pattern. |
| Your Turn! | Family Tree Drama | • To produce the language using the target grammar point in an imaginative context. |

| Unit 8 | Wh Questions. | Goal |
|---|---|---|
| Warm-Up | Identify | • For students to activate prior contents.<br>• For students to recognize the correct use of Wh Questions. |
| Let's Practice! | Role PLay Interviews | • For students to make correct and active use of Wh Questions.<br>• For students to practice question asking.<br>• For students to gain confidence by interacting with others using the target language. |
| Your Turn! | Whodunit Mystery | • For students to consolidate making the correct use of Wh questions in an engaging and more free way. |

# UNIT 1: ...AND ACTION! (VERBS)

Look at the pictures and try to write the correct verb under it.

think

**Let's Practice!**

**Verbs Charades:** Get in groups. One member of each group goes to the front, picks a card that will contain a verb and acts it. The rest of the group members of each team must guess what verb is it.

The team that guesses the most verbs wins!

You can get the cards from the back of your book (p. 45-53).

**act:**
do something, perform

I GIVE THIS ACTIVITY:

MY FAVORITE PART WAS:

**Your Turn!**

**Action Verbs Skit:** Work in groups. Choose 5 different action verbs. Each group must create a short story using those verbs and then perform it. The audience must identify which verbs are present in your story.

# UNIT 2: PRONOUNS AND SENTENCE STRUCTURE

**Warm-up** — Read the following text. Choose your favorite color and identify all the **subject pronouns** you can find.

Eva and Suzzie are twins, they are 10 years old and in fourth grade.

Eva and Suzzie do everything together; they are in the same class, they dress alike. They look the same. People always get them confused, which makes Eva and Suzzie laugh. Even their father has trouble telling them apart. Not their mother though.

Their older brother, Brad, is fifteen. He never knows which one is which. He doesn't even try.

One day, their father wanted to do different haircuts to Eva and Suzzie, to make it easy to know who is who, but the girls were horrified because they didn't want to look different!

So their mother came to the rescue and let them stay the same. They knew which one was which, and that was all that mattered.

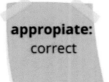

✦ Let's Practice! ✦

**Make sentences:** Look at the picture. Write sentences using the appropiate pronouns to describe the different scenes happening.

ex. Jessica holds the baby. *She* wears a yellow t-shirt.

**perform:**
act

**Your turn!**

**Creation Time**: Work in groups. Create your own picture and then perform it as a frozen image (tableau) so your classmates have to say what they see. Remember to use appropiate pronouns and sentence structure.

The audience should say things like: *"He walks/ He is walking, She ..../ She is ...."*

# UNIT 3: NOUNS IN THE SENTENCE

**Warm-up** — Look at the picture below. How many nouns can you identify? Find as much as you can in 5 minutes!

ex. (a) house

**Nouns Alphabet:** Everybody make a circle. Start with a letter of the alphabet, and each participant has to say a noun that starts with that letter. Continue until you've gone through the whole alphabet. If you don't know what to say, you step out of the circle.

I GIVE THIS ACTIVITY: ☆ ☆ ☆ ☆ ☆

MY FAVORITE PART WAS:

**without:**
not using,
not doing

**Nouns Acrostic Poem**: Choose one noun, anything you want, and then fill it with different nouns. Then in pairs, without showing what you wrote, draw one by one the nouns you used to build the poem. Make your partner try to guess the main word from your poem.

**Your turn!**

**For example:** Sky is the word your partner must guess, and     salt, kite, and yawn are the words you have to express with gestures or drawing!

**Salt**

**Kite**

**Yawn**

**enhanced:** make it better

# UNIT 4: LET'S USE ADJECTIVES!

**Warm-up**

**Adjective Transformation:** Look at these basic sentences; transform them by adding descriptive adjectives. For example, "*She walked in the park*" can become "*She walked happily in the beautiful park.*" Underline the adjective you add.

Act 2 or 3 sentences; tell your classmates the basic sentence, then act while your classmates guess the enhanced sentence.

It rains in the winter.

_____

The dog is barking.

_____

They live in a house.

_____

He is my friend.

_____

I have breakfast in the morning.

_____

**Adjective Swap:** Look at the dialogue; it has adjectives that have been erased. Read the dialogue and then work in groups to add appropriate adjectives to describe the characters and the situation.

After editing, perform the completed dialogue.

**John:** I have a _____ playdate tomorrow.

**Daniel:** Is it at the usual spot?

**John:** Yes, at my friend's _____ house.

**Daniel:** I heard it's a _____ playtime.

**John:** Yep, with toys and games!

**Daniel:** Are you _____?

**John:** Totally! I have my favorite snacks too.

**Daniel:** Awesome! It sounds like a _____ playdate.

**John:** Absolutely, and it starts at 2 PM.

**Adjective Storytelling:** Choose three adjectives and create a short story that has those adjectives.

Perform your story, making sure to highlight the adjectives in your narrative. At the end of your performance, the audience must identify the three adjectives you used.

**Your turn!**

Title:

# UNIT 5: USING ARTICLES

**Warm-up**

**Dialogues:** In the back of your book (p.54) there are three short dialogues that have article mistakes. Cut it and in couples, try to spot these mistakes, and then share them with the class.

**Glue the dialogues here**

**place:**
put in

*Let's Practice!*

**Article Hunt:** In the back of your book (p. 56–60), there are three short scripts that don't have some articles. In groups, choose one, cut it and identify where articles should be placed and write them in. Then act it out!

**Glue the script here**

**Character Descriptions**: Create short character descriptions. Choose or create a character of your choice.

In your description, you should use articles and adjectives to specify the characteristics of each character (e.g., "**The** *tall* and *mysterious* detective," "**A** *friendly* and *talkative* parrot," "**An** *evil* witch with a *crooked nose*").

After completing your descriptions, perform it to the class so they guess the character you chose.

**Your turn!**

**passing:**
giving

# UNIT 6: 1, 2, 3...
# SINGULARS AND PLURALS

**Warm-up**

**Singular/Plural Relay:**

In the back of your book (p. 62), there is a list of singular nouns. Get in groups, and in relay race fashion, each member of the group must run to the board and write the plural form of the noun before passing the marker to the next student.

The team that correctly writes the most plural nouns wins!

I GIVE THIS ACTIVITY:  ☆ ☆ ☆ ☆ ☆

MY FAVORITE PART WAS:

28

**Let's Practice!**

**Singular/Plural Mix-Up:** Look at the following sentences; they have singular and plural nouns mistakes. Rearrange the sentences to have the correct form and then perform the revised sentences.

A cats play in the yard.

_____

The child are playing in the park.

_____

She bought a new chairs.

_____

He has two car.

_____

The bird on the tree are singing.

_____

There are three computer in the office.

_____

The elephants in the zoo is enormous.

_____

**turns:** becomes

**Plural Storytelling:** In couples, choose a singular noun (e.g., "pencil," "tree") and create a short story about the change from singular to plural. For example, a story about a tree that magically turns into a forest.

After you create it, act out your story.

**Your turn!**

Title:

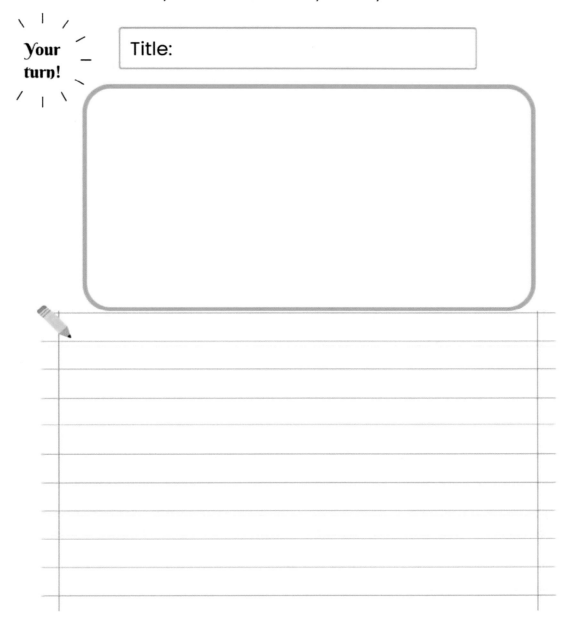

# UNIT 7: THE SPECIAL BE (VERB 'BE')

**Warm-up**

**Guess the Role:** Choose a role using "be" sentences. For example: *I am...* a teacher, a doctor, a mother.

In couples, ask each other yes-or-no questions to guess your identities (e.g., "Am I a teacher?" "Are we friends?").

Who are you?

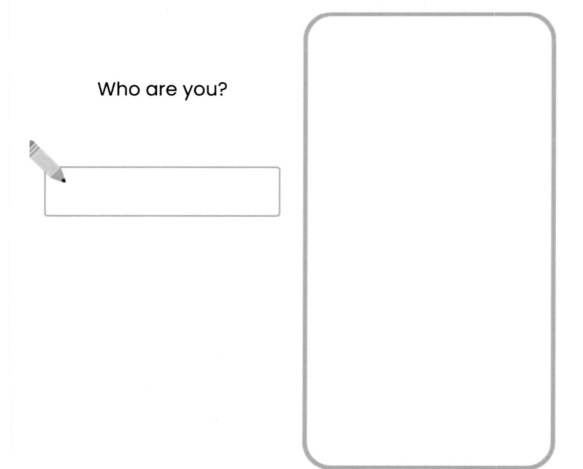

**Character Descriptions:** Choose a character, anyone or anything you want to be. Below, there's a description chart that will help you to write details about the character you chose (name, age, appearance, personality).

Complete the chart, and then after everyone has finished, one by one introduce yourselves as the characters you created. You must use "be" sentences (e.g., "I am John. I am 25 years old, and I am tall and friendly").

\ | /
**Let's**
**Practice!**
/ | \

| Name | |
|------|---|
| Age | |
| Appearance | |
| Personality | |

**fictional:** not real

**Family Tree Drama:** In groups of 5 or 6, create a family tree for a fictional family.
Each student takes on the role of a family member and uses "be" sentences to describe their relationships (e.g., "I am the son of Mary and John. My sister is Emily").

**Your turn!**

Family name:

# UNIT 8: WH QUESTIONS

**Identify:** Look at the following pictures. Fill each blank with *where, how, what, who, when.*

**Warm-up**

_____is this?

_____are you?

_____are we?

_____is the concert?

_____can I fix this?

**Role Play Interviews:** Choose a character or role.

Pair up, mingle and take turns interviewing each other using WH questions.

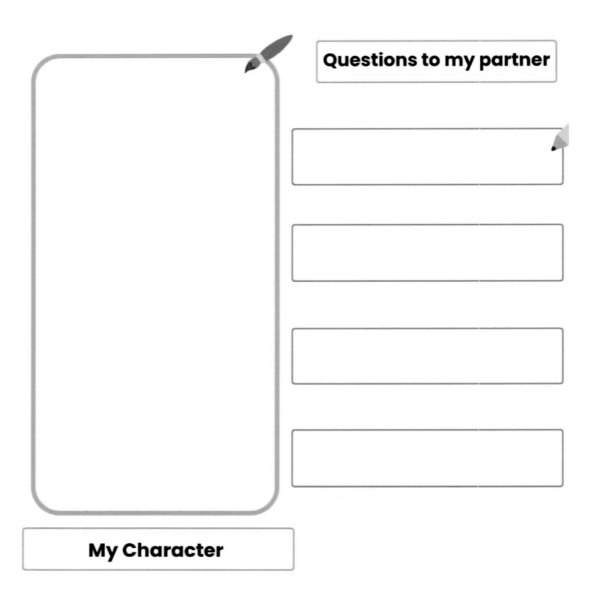

**Let's Practice!**

You must respond in character, providing detailed and relevant information.

For example, you can be a doctor, a model, or even a dog!

**Questions to my partner**

**My Character**

# WHODUNIT MYSTERY

## The Missing Cake

**Story:**

Yesterday was Mrs. Johnson's birthday, and she had baked a delicious chocolate cake for herself. She left it on the kitchen table to cool, but when she came back, the cake was missing! Mrs. Johnson is very sad and wants to know who took her birthday cake.

There are three suspects...Can you find who took Mrs. Johnson's birthday cake?

**Whodunit Mystery:** Poor Mrs. John... Let's help her find her birthday cake!

Everyone will play detectives who are trying to solve the case. The teacher is the only one who knows the details of the case that will help you to find who did it, but you have to ask the right questions!

**Your turn!**

**Write here your questions and notes to gather clues to solve the mystery**

ex. Who are the three suspects?

# FINAL PROJECT IDEAS

Now that you have finished this book, I hope you were able to master these basic grammar points. In order to prove so, it can be a great idea to have a final project where you can make use of everything you learned. Do you accept the challenge? (The teacher will help you all the time! So ask as much as you want)

**Project Idea 1: Put on your own "Puppet Show".**

Here are two folklore stories, one from South Korea and the other from Greece, which is known worldwide! With your group, choose one story and turn it into a puppet show. You have to make the stage (for example, you can make it with a carton box!), assign characters and craft your puppets (for example, you can use old socks, thick paper, fabric, etc.) Let your imagination flow! After having everything prepared, practice your lines and present it to the class.

*Story Nº 1: "The Boy Who Cried Wolf" (Greek story)*

Once upon a time, in a small village, there was a young boy named Jack. Jack had the job of watching over the village's sheep. His job was essential because wolves often roamed nearby, and the sheep needed protection.

One day, as Jack was sitting on a hill, he got a mischievous idea. He thought it would be funny to trick the villagers. So, he cried out loudly, "Wolf! Wolf! The wolf is coming!"

Hearing the boy's cries, the villagers quickly dropped what they were doing and rushed to the fields with sticks and stones, ready to chase away the wolf. However, when they arrived, they found no wolf. Jack just laughed and said, "I fooled you!"

The villagers weren't pleased, but they went back to their work, thinking it was just a joke. However, Jack found the trick amusing and decided to try it again.

A few days later, Jack spotted a real wolf approaching the flock. This time, he was genuinely scared. He shouted, "Wolf! Wolf! The wolf is coming! Help!"

But this time, the villagers, remembering the previous false alarm, didn't believe him. They thought it was another one of Jack's tricks, so they stayed in the village, ignoring his cries for help.

Sadly, the wolf attacked the sheep, and Jack learned a valuable lesson. Lying and tricking others can lead to serious consequences. From that day on, Jack regretted his actions, and the villagers learned to be cautious when someone cried for help.

The moral of the story is: Always tell the truth, and people will trust you when you really need help.

# FINAL PROJECT IDEAS

### *Story Nº 2: The Rabbit's Liver (Korean folk tale)*

Once upon a time, in the deep sea, there were four dragon kings, each taking care of their own special part under the water. The dragon king in charge of the southern sea became very sick. A magical being from the heavenly kingdom came down to visit the sick king.

"I traveled from heaven after hearing that you're not feeling well," said the divine old man. He drew a picture of a rabbit for the sick king before disappearing.

The sea court officials were puzzled when they learned that the rabbit lived on land. But then a wise turtle stepped forward.
"I will find the rabbit," declared the turtle.

With the drawing in hand, the turtle swam towards the shore. As it reached land, the turtle wondered, "Where could this rabbit be?"
Suddenly, a fluffy white creature hopped down from the mountain. The turtle called out to the rabbit.
"No, I can't go so far! I don't even know how to swim," replied the rabbit.

"Don't worry. You can ride on my back, and I'll take you to the sea palace. I promise to bring you back whenever you want."
Afraid that the rabbit might change his mind, the turtle swam quickly to the sea palace with the rabbit on his back.

Soldiers tried to carry the rabbit to the dragon king's chamber, but the rabbit, feeling scared, said, "My liver is not here right now. We always hide it when we go out because everyone wants our livers." The rabbit promised to bring back his liver and returned with the turtle to the land.

"Let's go get your liver," said the turtle.
"You believed that story? What animal can take out its liver and still live?" laughed the rabbit as he ran away. The turtle sat there for a long time, crying.

But then the rabbit came back with a big load of rabbit poop. The turtle carefully wrapped the poop and brought it back to the sea palace. The dragon king ate the poop and magically became healthy again.

As a reward, the turtle was given a high court position, and everyone lived happily ever after. The end.

# FINAL PROJECT IDEAS

**Project Idea 2: Create a "Story Telling".**

With your group, create a short story based on one of the two tittles below. After making the story, assign characters and practice the scenes. Try wearing costumes (using things you have at home!), and perform your story. How fun!

The Talking Tree

Lost in the Forest

**Create a "Story Telling": Here you have lines to write your story.**

**Create a "Story Telling": Here you have lines to write your story.**

# APPENDIX: MATERIALS

✂ **Unit 1: Let's practice – Verbs Charades Cards**

| | |
|---|---|
| **Play** | **Think** |
| **Sleep** | **Make** |
| **Break** | **Buy** |

# APPENDIX: MATERIALS

✂ **Unit 1: Let's practice - Verbs Charades Cards**

| | |
|---|---|
| **Catch** | **Come** |
| **Dance** | **Choose** |
| **Run** | **Draw** |

# APPENDIX: MATERIALS

Unit 1: Let's practice - Verbs Charades Cards

| | |
|---|---|
| **Climb** | **Eat** |
| **Go** | **Dream** |
| **Look** | **Write** |

# APPENDIX: MATERIALS

Unit 1: Let's practice - Verbs Charades Cards (Add your own verbs)

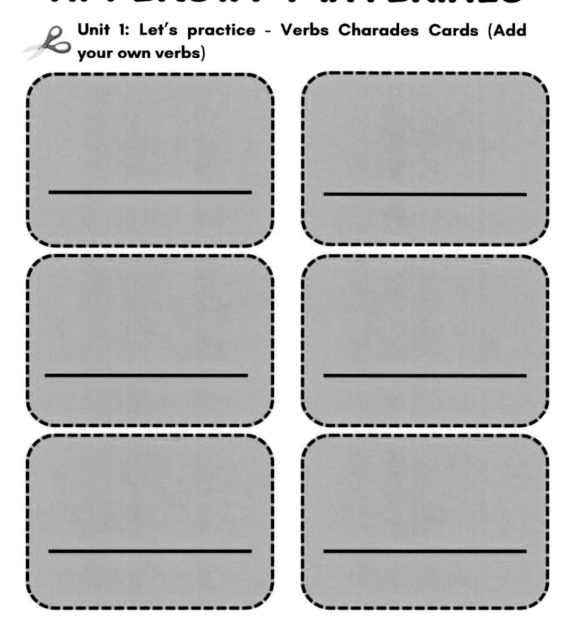

# APPENDIX: MATERIALS

 **Unit 5: Warm Up - Dialogues**

## Dialogue 1
Person A: "I'm going to an store. Need anything?"
Person B: "Yes, I need milk and bread."
Person A: "Okay, I'll get it for you."

## Dialogue 2
Person A: "I saw a interesting movie last night."
Person B: "Oh, really? What was it about?"
Person A: "It was about detective who solves an mystery."

## Dialogue 3
Person A: "I have a appointment with doctor tomorrow."
Person B: "I hope it's nothing serious."
Person A: "I'm not sure. But I'll discuss with a doctor."

# APPENDIX: MATERIALS

 **Unit 5: Let's Practice! - Article Hunt**

**Script 1: A Day in Park**

Lisa and Mike are discussing their plans for the day.
LISA: I want to go to park.
MIKE: Oh, that sounds fun! We can have picnic.
LISA: Yes! I have blanket in car.

They head to the car.

Lisa and Mike arrive at the park.
MIKE: Look at those kids playing on swings.
LISA: Let's join them!

They approach the swings.

MIKE: I haven't been on swings in years.
LISA: It's never too late!

They laugh and enjoy swinging.

LISA: This reminds me of time we went amusement park.
MIKE:Oh, I remember. We rode roller coaster.
LISA: And ate cotton candy.

They continue reminiscing.

MIKE: I miss those days.
LISA: Me too. We should plan another trip.

They leave the park.

# APPENDIX: MATERIALS

 **Unit 5: Let's Practice! - Article Hunt**

**Script 2: Lost Keys**

Anna is frantically searching for her keys.
ANNA: I can't find keys anywhere!

TOM: (enters the room) Did you check table?

ANNA: Yes, I looked on table, in kitchen, and bedroom.

TOM: Maybe keys fell behind sofa.

They search behind the sofa.

ANNA: No, not there. I need keys for car.

TOM: We can retrace steps. Where were you before?

ANNA: I was in store, then at friend's house.

TOM: Did you check car?

ANNA: Not yet. Let's go check car.

They head to the garage.

ANNA: Here they are!

TOM:I told you to check car!

They both laugh.

# APPENDIX: MATERIALS

 **Unit 5: Let's Practice! - Article Hunt**

**Script 3: Morning Rush**

Alex is running late for work, searching for breakfast.
ALEX: I need cereal, milk, and coffee.

Jen, Alex's roommate, enters the kitchen.

JEN: Why you in hurry?

ALEX: Late for meeting. Can't find coffee filters.

JEN: Did you check cupboard?

ALEX: Yes, not there.

JEN: What about fridge?

ALEX: Good idea!

They check the fridge.

ALEX: No milk either.

JEN: I have milk in my fridge.

ALEX: Thanks! I'll get it from there.

JEN: You also need banana.

ALEX: Oh, you're right! Thanks for help!

Alex rushes out the door.

# APPENDIX: MATERIALS

Unit 6: Warm Up - Singular/ Plural Relay

## List of Singular Nouns

1. Picture
2. Teacher
3. Student
4. Friend
5. Garden
6. Bike
7. Beach
8. Star
9. Cup
10. Plate
11. Toothbrush
12. Elephant
13. Giraffe
14. Mouse
15. Doctor
16. Nurse
17. Key
18. Bed
19. Sunflower
20. Umbrella
21. Phone
22. Pizza
23. Elephant
24. Moon
25. Shirt

# SELF EVALUATION

And... here is the end of this book! You have made an amazing job. I hope you had fun while learning these important grammar points. Now, it is time to be very HONEST, and check how much did you learn.

| Can I...? | Yes, I can | I can, but I need more practice | No, I cannot |
|---|---|---|---|
| Recognize, identify, and use action verbs | | | |
| Make a simple sentence | | | |
| Understand and use pronouns | | | |
| Recognize and use nouns | | | |
| Recognize and use adjectives | | | |
| Recognize and use the correct articles | | | |
| Recognize and understand singular and plural nouns | | | |
| Ask questions using Wh words | | | |

**Make a final comment:**

# THANK YOU FOR USING THIS BOOK, SEE YOU IN THE NEXT LEVEL!

# EPILOGUE

As you witnessed through the different units present in this book, the main goal of each unit was for students to make actual use of the grammar point they were learning. And of course, the demand and difficulty of activities increase through the passing of units.

As I mentioned on the prior page, I will see you again in the next book! Because that is right... Learning Grammar with Drama is a book series!

And this is not the end of it! I am planning to extend drama techniques into other language areas and contents! I hope I can meet you there too. Until then!